Improving Your
& People Skills Gu

C000301213

77 Tricks on How to Improve Your Conversational Skills, Increase
Self-Worth, Become More Confident and Speak Effectively. A
Book Guide Perfect for Teens or Adults

A.V. Mendez

Copyright © 2020 A.V. Mendez

All rights reserved. No part of this publication may be reproduced, stored in a retrieval system, or transmitted in any form or by any means, without the prior permission in writing from the publisher.

The publisher is not responsible for websites (or their content) that are not owned by the publisher.

TABLE OF CONTENTS

OTHER BOOKS

The 45-Day Self Improvement Handbook: 45 Daily Ideas, Habits and Action-Plan for Becoming More Productive, Persuasive, Influential, Sociable and Self- Confident

Build Confidence & Self-Esteem: 90 Awesome Techniques to Become Confident, Overcome Self-Doubt, Shyness and Improve Your Self-Esteem

How to Focus: 54 Habits, Tools and Ideas to Create Superhuman Focus, Eliminate Distractions, Stop Procrastination and Achieve More With Less Work

Stop Procrastination & Increase Productivity: 60 Tricks on How to Improve Your Focus, Time Management, Habits, Productivity and Overall Ability to Get Things Done

Introduction

Imagine being able to connect with anyone. Imagine being able to talk to people with ease - no awkwardness, just the pure joy of having a conversation. Imagine being able to understand other people quickly. To know how they feel and communicate in a way that makes them like you.

Well, you don't have to imagine anymore. In this book, I am going to show you 77 easy to apply methods that will help you improve your social skills.

Methods that will range from "learning how to listen well" to "knowing how to approach a conversation." All of the lessons here can be applied in your daily life. These are all "street level" tactics that anyone can do.

The ideas doesn't require some rocket scientist to apply.

How to Use the Book

Every idea consists of 2 parts. The first one is the explanation of the idea and its importance in terms of social skill improvement. The second part shows you the *action guide* where I will give you some things to do so you can apply the idea immediately.

The first part shows the idea and the second part gives you a plan of action that you can do to start implementing the lessons from that chapter.

4 Benefits of Having *Social & People Skills*

Before we start, allow me to mention the top 4 benefits of learning how to improve your social skills. How can improving your social skills help you in life? What are the things that are going to change for you if you implement the lessons inside this book?

1 - Advancing Career Prospects

The better you are at communicating with other people, the more you are likely to get opportunities for advancing your career. People who know how to connect with other people are usually the ones promoted to higher positions in the corporate world.

2 - Sell More Stuff

If you're an entrepreneur, improving your social skills means you're going to sell more product and services. The better you are at communicating the value of your product, the more of it you will sell.

3 - Influence People

Whether you're a manager, a coach, a consultant, or whatever your job is, influencing people will always be part of the game. You're going to have to convince people to *buy in*. You're going to have to sell your vision. You're going to have to give them a reason to follow your lead.

4 - Have Better Relationships

People who know how to communicate well are usually the ones with the happiest relationships.

Understanding yourself and other people in terms of communication means you'll know how to act around people. It means you'll be able to understand your partner well. It means you'll be able to know why the people around you act a certain way.

Personally, I think that this is the best benefit of having *maximum social skills*. It's the ability to understand other people around you.

Look, you don't have to be a master communicator in 3 months. That's impossible to do. But you have to commit to learning and improving every day. If you do that, you won't even recognize yourself (in a good way) 6-12 months from now.

With that said, expect some bumps along the way but don't let it stop you from becoming a better communicator and conversationalist.

Let's get started.

Part 1
Fears, Goals
and Empathy

1 - Overcome Your Fears

First things first, you have to overcome your fears of talking to other people. I know, it isn't as easy as it sounds - but you do have to do it. You have to have the courage to approach other people. You have to have the courage to put yourself out there.

If not, then there's no way you are going to be a better communicator. You can't be a better conversationalist if you're just sitting all day in front of your computer.

You can't be timid. You have to take the initiative to talk to other people. You have to surround yourself with people you like to talk to.

So how do you do that? How do you overcome your fear of talking to people? How do you overcome your fear of getting embarrassed?

Well, you start small. You start with looking people in the eye, then you learn how to say hi, then you start learning when to nod…. And so on. The key is to start with something that you can easily do. For some, the starting point would be learning how to nod. For some, it will be learning how to say hi. These are little things that anyone can do to get started.

If your goal is to learn how to become a charismatic leader, then you're going to have to start small. Start with whatever you can do in order to move forward.

Action Guide:

1 - Overcome your fear by starting small. Start with some of the easiest things you can do.

2 - I recommend that you do this exercise.

A - Go to a convenience store and ask for something. A pack of ice is the best one to ask since most convenience stores pack their ice in the back of the store - it's something that you won't see immediately.

B - Buy one pack and do not pay in the exact amount. By doing this, you'll have more time in there, thus helping you get more comfortable with the *silence gap* of waiting for the change.

C - Once the cashier gave the change, look her in the eye, say "thanks" and leave.

This simple exercise can help you overcome your initial fear of having a conversation. I know that this may seem too simple for some. But for others who have troubles with their social skills, I would say that this is a good starting point. Do it and see the results for yourself.

2 - Expect to Mess Up at Times

I wish I could tell you that every conversation that you'll have will be smooth and free-flowing. I wish I could tell you that you won't ever make mistakes - say the wrong things or react the wrong way.

But the truth is, you are going to mess up at times. You are going to have the wrong body language. You are going to say the wrong things. You are going to be insensitive.

Those things are going to happen. And when it does, the best way to deal with it is to learn from it and move on.

Don't kick yourself for making a mistake. Acknowledge what you did, apologize to the other person if you have to, learn your lessons and avoid making the same mistake again.

Action Guide:

1 - Go back to your last few conversations. Are there things you wish you didn't do? Words you wish you haven't said? Go write those "mistakes" in a piece of paper and write what you could've done better. The goal of this exercise is not to sulk on your mistakes. The goal is to learn from it so you never have to make the same mistake ever again. If you get a lesson for every mistake that you make, that makes the mistake less painful and more beneficial to you.

3 - Mirror, Mirror on the Wall

If you're an introvert like me, then you probably have a hard time starting a conversation. You're too conscious with what you'll say that you pretty much mess up with words all the time.

If possible, you can practice talking to yourself in the mirror before having a conversation with someone.

Usually, I practice what I would say or I role play as if I'm already talking to the other person. This idea may seem a little crazy but it's something that works for me.

You have to do everything you can in order to be comfortable while having a conversation. If you feel restless, then it will show and it'll make the other person feel uncomfortable.

Remember, your energy almost always reflects the energy of your conversation partner. If you're excited, then excitement also emboldens the other person. If you're timid and tired, this will also reflect to the other person and he will act timid and tired as well.

Action Guide:

1 - Practice having a conversation with yourself in the mirror. Pump yourself up and then practice what you have to say to the other person.

2 - Remember that people tend to mirror our energy. If you want the conversation to be lively, then act happy and excited. If you

want the conversation to be serious, then act serious and say things straight to the point.

4 - Set A Conversation Goal

The majority of meetings are a waste of time. Why? Because people who run them usually don't have a conversation goal.

It's the same with most of our conversations. We should have the aim to get something out of it.

These goals could be the following:

-To find a solution to a problem
-To catch up with each other's stories
-To brainstorm business ideas
-To have fun and just talk about anything

Whatever that goal is, you have to have that in your mind so you don't have to waste time on conversations that don't have any aim.

Now, if your goal is to just catch up with a friend, then that is perfectly fine. At least, you have a goal that is in the back of your mind. Now, for more serious matters like finding a solution to a problem, you have to identify the problem and then think of solutions that you and your conversation partner can do to solve it.

Having that goal makes the conversation more focused, and it helps you in not wasting any time talking about things that have nothing to do with your goal. This makes the conversation more effective and efficient for both of you.

Action Guide:

1 - Set a goal for the conversation. What do you have to get out of this conversation? Why are you having this conversation in the first place? Having that goal helps you to not be side-tracked and talk about random stuff. This also saves you time that you can use instead on more important tasks.

2 - Before the start of the conversation (especially for more serious ones), mention to the other person the goal for that meeting. By doing this, both of you won't lose focus on what you are supposed to be talking about.

5 - Ask Good Questions

Not all questions are created equal.

There are questions that don't serve any purpose and there are questions that helps the conversation move forward.

Now, these questions will be based mostly on your topic. A good question about topic X may be considered as a bad question on topic Y.

So how do you formulate good questions? What questions should you ask to move the conversation on the right path?

First of all, you have to ask questions that serves a purpose. You have to ask yourself. What is the purpose of this question? Why are you asking it in the first place?

Second, you have to know if it's an appropriate question while thinking of the context of the situation.

For example, let's suppose that you are having trouble with a staff member. The problem is she always comes late and it's already driving you crazy. You wanted to fire her already but you want to give her another chance. Now, there are two ways to approach this. You can either say:

A - "Lany, you always come late and if you do that again, then I'm gonna have to fire you. Do you have problems with waking up early or something?"

Or

B – "Lany, I notice in the past few days that you always came late, now this is already affecting your productivity. Is there something I can help you with so this doesn't happen again? Is there something that you want to tell me why you're struggling with this issue? I would really appreciate your honesty."

What do you think is the better response and question? The first one or the second one?

To me, it's the second one. Why? Because it comes from a place of help and understanding. It is not brash and it's not condescending.

Having the second one as your response will give you a better understanding of why your staff is acting that way.

Action Guide:

1 - Look at the issues that you are having lately. Possible issues with your partner, employees, friends, and colleagues.

2 - Identify the problem and ask yourself. How can I solve this problem? What question may I ask other people that can help solve this issue? How can you approach this in a way that doesn't condescend other people?

3 - Have the courage to actually have a potentially uncomfortable conversation. Just make sure that you come from a place of help and understanding.

6 - Watch Out for Their Interest

People are selfish. They like to talk about themselves. They like to talk about things that interest them.

They don't care about your day, they don't care about your promotion, and they don't care about how many employees of the month awards you got this year.

This may seem like a pessimistic way to look at it, but it's the reality. Most people just don't care that much about us. And this is actually good news for us! That means we can talk less and listen more. That means we can talk about them instead of ourselves. Now, everyone, including us wants to talk about ourselves - so you have to fight the urge to talk about yourself. You have to fight the urge to brag about your achievements.

We have to focus on the other person. We have to focus on what they want to talk about - which most of the time, is themselves.

This is not about being an "as*kisser." It's about understanding the other person's wants and desires. It's about realizing that most people want to talk about themselves.

Take advantage of this fact and focus on them.

Action Guide:

1 - The first thing I always want to know about a person is their interests. What do they want to talk about? What are the topics that make them feel alive? You can start by asking questions like:

A - What is your favorite thing to do on weekends?

B - Do you have a hobby that you're passionate about?

2 - Once they start talking about a certain topic, you'll easily know if they're passionate about it or not. Don't interrupt them. Don't try to give your take early in the conversation. Just let them talk about stuff they're interested in as much as they can.

3 - I try to follow this structure in my conversations. **70%-80% listening, 20%-30% talking**. Obviously, I don't count how many times I speak. I just listen as much as I can and I talk whenever the other person asks about something. If the conversation ends and I felt like I listened more than I talked, then that's good enough for me.

7 - Acknowledge Their Point

Look, you don't have to agree to everything your conversation partner says. You don't have to say that they are right all the time. But you do have to do something that will make them more likely to respect your position.

And that is to acknowledge their point. Acknowledging something doesn't mean you're agreeing with it. Acknowledging something means you're giving that statement and that person the respect they deserve. It means that you're open to changing your mind but they still have to defend that idea better.

Let's suppose that you guys are talking about whether The Walking Dead Season 9 is good or bad. So your friend said, "I hate TWD season 9, without Rick Grimes, Walking Dead is just not the same." The goal of your response is not to change his mind. The goal of your response is to acknowledge what they feel and then add your own take on it. So your response could sound something like this: "Yeah, I get you. Rick Grimes is the main protagonist of the show and he can never ever be replaced. I wish they would bring him back in the future. And I do think that they did a better job this season in terms of storytelling, they let Daryl shine and they gave him more lines to say so that made season 9 better for me."

Instead of saying "Nah, season 9 is good and you're just dumb," you can have a better conversation by acknowledging what the other person feels at first. You're not agreeing with your friend but you're also acknowledging his point. And that's enough for him to respect your position and make your conversation more stimulating.

Action Guide:

1 - Do not disagree with the other person in a direct manner. Acknowledge their point and consider their feelings. Unless you're having a debate, then the purpose of the conversation is not to know who is right. The purpose of the conversation is to let each other's opinion be heard.

2 - Avoid the word BUT if possible. You can replace it with words like *and, in addition, plus,* and *also.*

8 - Avoid Arguments

In his article "It's not enough to be right, you also have to be kind," Ryan Holiday discuss how we as a generation, has become obsessed with the idea of being right.

We tend to make assumptions that just because the other person disagrees with us, we tend to label the other person with words like "racist, sexist, or worse - Nazi."

We don't even try to understand the other person anymore. We just assume things. For us, being right is better than being kind. This brings in more argument and more clever quips against each other.

It doesn't really bring anything to the table but chaos.

As Ryan said: *"I thought if I was just overwhelmingly right enough, I could get people to listen."* But they don't and they won't. Avoid the arguments if possible. Learn to defend your position by stating facts. Learn to defend your position by understanding what the other person feels. It's not just about "Facts over feelings." It's also about FACTS & FEELINGS. They are equally important and equally requires an important examination.

Action Guide:

1 - Read Ryan Holiday's article about the topic.

https://medium.com/s/story/its-not-enough-to-be-right-you-also-have-to-be-kind-b8814111fe1

2 - Examine how you react about things. Especially the topics where you disagree with what the other person is saying. Ask yourself, do you really have to mention your clever quips just to sound right? Or is the best solution at the moment is to shut up and listen?

3 - Avoid the arguments and only take on them when necessary. Necessary is when you're in a setting like debates, meetings, and the corporate environment when you have to create a solution for the problem that your company is experiencing.

9 - Mention and Remember Their Name

The best sound in the world will always be the sound of your name. Whenever someone mentions our name, we can't help but look. It's a sweet sound - and we love hearing it. Use people's name in all the communication that you have. Whether it's email, text, messenger or whatever platform you use, use their name as much as possible.

This brings trust subconsciously. They can't help it. People will trust someone who knows and never forgets their name.

Also, try not to botch the spelling and the pronunciation of their name. You are not a Starbucks barista. It's all fun and games when you're at a coffee shop, but in a more professional setting, botching someone's name could mean being laughed at or picked on by co-workers.

Action Guide:

1 - Use other people's name in every chance that you'll get. Just make sure you're talking about something positive.

2 - Never, ever forget someone's name. Even if you only met a person once, try to take note of his or her name by associating them with something. Let's say that her name is France. Then just think about the country of France when she gets introduced to you. If his name is Mark, think about an X mark when you look at him. Associating their name with something really helps your brain remember the name, thus making you less likely to forget about it.

10 - Empathize

Empathizing with someone means trying to understand where someone is coming from. What is the context behind his or her statements? Why does he believe a certain thing even though the facts suggest otherwise?

Instead of having clever quips and airing an authority of moral superiority, try to understand the other person instead. You don't have to agree with everything they say. But you do have to understand why they believe what they believe.

For example, let's say a new friend of yours believe that Marxism and communism is the solution to the world's problems. Ask the person why he believed so. Listen carefully so you can find out why he believes what he believes.

By doing this, you'll understand the other person better. Then you can start acknowledging his points, and then start adding your own take why you believe otherwise.

Action Guide:

1 - Before you judge a person and their ideas, try to understand the context first. Does she have some kind of personal experience that makes her a little biased in her argument? Did she study this topic all her life, thus making her an authority and a valid defender of the argument? Know what it feels like to be them and understand their own biases and personal experience.

2 - Be open to changing your mind. Unless you have all the facts, and you 100% believe that you are right, then changing your mind about a specific topic doesn't make you any less smart.

3 - Create an environment of decent conversation. The problem with politics nowadays is that the left and the right are mostly just jabbing at each other. By having a conversation based on mutual respect for each other's opinion, we will be able to have a better understanding of each other's worldview.

Part 2
Practical Strategies for Improving Social Skills

11 - Avoid Fidgeting

One of the most annoying things you can do is to keep fidgeting while having a conversation. It's not only annoying but also distracting.

Fidgeting is a non-verbal sign that you are either:

Uncomfortable
Annoyed
Bored
Not focus on the topic
Don't care about the conversation

Your conversation partner may find your fidgeting to be any of these things.

What if you're having a conversation about him investing in your company? What if every time he talks, you keep clicking your pen on and off - isn't that super annoying? Isn't that going to make him feel uneasy?

These little actions may look nothing to us. It may look normal to us… but the truth is, they are non-verbal signals that may destroy your conversation.

Action Guide:

1 - Ask your friends about any habits that you have during a conversation. It could be getting a pen and clicking it on and off, or touching your nose every few seconds, or shaking your legs.

2 - Stop yourself immediately whenever you find yourself doing these annoying habits. Remember, they're just bad habits. You can still change them - but it could be a little hard to do if you've been doing them for years. So try to change them little by little. You don't have to be perfect at it in the beginning. Just learn to be aware of your fidgeting habits and quickly force yourself to stop once you catch yourself doing them.

12 - Find Your People

Why is it hard to talk to strangers? The obvious reason is that you don't know each other. That means you have no idea about his name, his experience, his job, and his interests.

So you have to find your own people. You have to find people who have the same interests as you do. "Your People" are the people in your field of interest. If you're a motorcycle enthusiast and you go to a moto meet-up, then it wouldn't be hard to start a conversation. You can talk to a stranger and just talk about bikes. By having a common interest, you already set yourself up for an easier conversation. If you're an introvert who doesn't like to talk to strangers, this can also be a good start for you. Just talk about something you already know a lot of things about. Talk to people who understand your passion. Talk to people who knows the lingo of your field. By doing this, most of the conversations you'll have will be easy.

Action Guide:

1 - Find where *your people* hang out. Search for possible places online on where they might be and what time and days do they go there.

2 - Introduce yourself and ask something about them. Ask how long have they been in the field. Ask anything that would make them talk all day long! The more passionate they are about the topic, the easier the conversation will be because you only have to talk 20% of the time.

13 - Encourage Others to Be Themselves

We live in a world where the external appearance matters a lot. You see it on Instagram & Facebook, magazine covers, movies, and television.

Someone buys a $200,000 car and it gets 570 likes. But what most people don't know is he got it by getting a 5-year loan that he can barely afford.

Some Insta model has 2 million followers but is broke as hell!

Instead of being true to themselves, people think that they just have to project a certain image for other people to like them. We want the validation. We want the praise.

In a world full of fake Influencers, be someone who encourages other people to be their best true self.

If your friend is broke and at around $10,000 in debt, then always remind him about the most important stuff. Remind him of his dreams. Remind him of his potential to do something great. Encourage other people to grow and to take action. We all need someone who will encourage us and assure us that, as long as we work hard and work smart, then our sacrifices will pay-off someday.

Action Guide:

1 - Are you or someone you know faking it online just to get other people's approval? Be honest, be real - live your truth and it will make you happier.

2 - Encourage other people to tell their truth. Encourage other people to accept their current reality, and then push them to take action and change it for the better.

14 - Art of Active Listening and Replying with Good Intent

Listening isn't about waiting for someone to finish talking so you can now give your own take about that certain topic. Listening is about intentionally understanding what the other person is saying, and then making a reply based on the content of what they said.

Active Listening

Here's the difference between active listening and the type of listening that most of us do today.

Active Listening looks like this:

Him: "Hey men, I got a problem at work, some girl keeps sending me creepy letters on my desk every morning"

You: "shiit, really, that's messed up! So what did you do?"

The normal type of listening that we do today looks like this:

Him: "Hey men, I got a problem at work, some girl keeps sending me creepy letters on my desk every morning"

You: "dude, we also have a weird girl in the office sending stickers to everyone almost every week"

Did you see the difference?

The difference is in the content of the reply. Active listening means you reply with the intent of finding out more about what he is saying. The second type of listening takes the focus away from the other person to you.

So if you think about it, active listening means understanding the other person and not trying to steal their thunder! Active listening means knowing the right things to say while still making them the focus of the conversation.

Action Guide:

1 - On your next conversation, focus on what the other person is saying instead of what you're about to say. You don't have to sound smart or look smarter than the other person. You just have to learn how to actively listen so you can then give a genuine reply with the intent of making them, still the focus of the conversation.

2 - When replying to a statement made by your conversation partner, make sure that you're not focusing on your own experience. Keep asking them questions related to their original statement. When he asked about your stories or opinion about it, that's when you start making the conversation a little more about you - but that's only because the other person asked for it.

15 - Set Your Phone Aside

This has become an epidemic. We can't even spend 10 minutes without looking at our phones. There's a beautiful woman 12 feet away from you just waiting for someone to talk to her, yet there you are, fake typing something on your phone instead of approaching her. Go to a Starbucks near you and you'll find friends who are hyper-focus on their mobile devices while ignoring each other.

Look, I understand that the world is now different. That the world is now connected through our smartphones. But have we sacrificed our true personal connections so we can have millions of fake surface-level ones?

Why don't we bring it back old school sometimes? Let's set aside our phone sometimes - so we can finally have an honest to goodness conversation that will actually bring value to us.

Action Guide:

1 - Go to a coffee shop and notice how many friends are having conversations while they mostly look at their phone. This will give you a new perspective on how much time we are wasting and how unfocus our conversations has become.

2 - On your next conversation, tell the other person that you prefer to talk without holding your phone. Set both of your phones aside and have the classic conversation just like the old days! No phone, just you and the other person focused on each other's stories.

16 - Finding and Making the Right Friends

They say that we are the average of our 5 closest friends. I believe in this statement, and you should too.

I mean, go look at your own life. Go look at your house, your car, your income, and even your habits. I can almost guarantee you that it'll probably be the average of what your 5 closest friends have.

So do you want to make more money? Do you want to have a more successful business? Then either make new friends or level up with the friends that you currently have.

Social skills are not just about communicating with strangers. It's also about communicating with the right people. It's about having a conversation with people you like. By having friends you love and trust, the conversation becomes easier. The conversation becomes effortless.

So you have to find the right friends. First of all, are your current friends a good influence for you? Or are they mostly people who already gave up on life? I'm not saying that you should ditch your friends. No, in fact, you should try to help them level up too as much as you can. But their decisions and actions are not up to you. You can never force someone to make a change. You can only encourage them, educate them and make them believe in their capacity. But they themselves are the only ones who can improve their lives.

Action Guide:

1 - Remember that choosing the right friends to have a conversation with is also as important as having good communication skills.

2 - Choose your friends well. Make sure that you're having conversations that you find valuable. If all you guys do all they long are play video games and talk about vacations, then that friendship won't serve you well. It won't make you grow and it won't make you better.

3 - Find new friends who have the same interests as you do. The more you have in common, the easier the conversation will be.

17 - Give Compliments

I don't know why but I think that we have become afraid of noticing other people. We think that complimenting someone's dress may lead to sexual abuse accuse in the future... We think that other people will think that we need something because we compliment their output for this month's work... We're afraid that our compliments will lead to something negative.

But you shouldn't be afraid. You shouldn't stop giving compliments. If your intention is good - people will know, people will sense your genuineness.

Give compliments whenever possible. Did your staff finished all the tasks on time, send an email and let them know that you are sending pizza on the pantry. Did an officemate excel on her job this week?, then tell her how awesome she is by giving her a compliment. A simple "hey Lany, great job on the x process this week, I'll see ya on Monday" will go a long way!

Compliment other people, even in the smallest things that they do. They will appreciate it and they will like you more! Just be genuine in giving your compliments. You don't know how a simple compliment can change someone's day or week. Be the light that makes them shine and you'll start to notice that all these light ends up reflecting on you.

Action Guide:

1 - Compliment someone today. Give a genuine compliment and watch how other people shine.

18 - Learn to Excuse Yourself

This is an avoidance tactic and I do not recommend that you use this often. But sometimes, there's just no other way but to excuse yourself from the conversation.

Sometimes, you will feel too many negative emotions. The conversation isn't going your way and you feel pressured to say something smart. Thus, this only makes you say something stupid. In this case, you should've just excused yourself from the conversation.

Whenever the need arises to excuse yourself, then you got to have an exit strategy that you can use.

Here are some of my favorites:

"Hey bro, Imma just go to the restroom and I'll get back to you on your question"

"Mr. President, may I excuse myself as I need to use the restroom?"

Here's another one:

I'll grab my phone as if it vibrated and I'll look at the message app, then I'll excuse myself to answer a fake call. I know, this tactic seems dumb, but it works for me! If I don't have any choice, and the conversation already turned awkward and silent, I do this so others can take a break as well.

The secret is not in the words you say or things that you do. It's the act of being comfortable in excusing yourself. The truth is, the other people around you might need the break as well! You're not only doing yourself a favor, but you're also letting other people have an excuse to do something that they need to do (but are too shy to say something about it).

Action Guide:

1 - Practice excusing yourself from a conversation. Think of ways how to excuse yourself from a conversation in a respectful manner.

Here are the most common ones you can use:

1. "Did you see the restroom anywhere?"
2. "I think I left my [laptop/bag/phone] in the other room. I'd better go grab it before it disappears."
3. "I need another drink, what about you?"
4. "You love XYZ? You should meet Joe, he loves XYZ too!"
5. "Do you know anyone else here who has experience with/is interested in/could help with X?"
6. "Excuse me."
7. "I have a question I wanted to ask the speaker before s/he leaves."
8. "Anyway, I don't want to monopolize all your time."
9. "All right, I need to go check in with my team. It's been great chatting."
10. "So, listen, it's been great catching up with you. Let's exchange cards?"
11. "Hold on, I've got to take this."

Source: https://blog.hubspot.com/marketing/excuse-yourself-conversation-gracefully

19 - Save Them from Other People

Not all of the conversations we'll have will turn out positive. There are moments where we'll see someone get uncomfortable because of the topic. There are conversations where the clash of different opinions may lead to shouting and more disagreements. This is where we come in. We can be the Knight in shining armor who can salvage the conversation. We can be the voice of reason so people will start to calm down and start being reasonable again. By becoming this type of person, you're basically giving an air of authority in a natural way. You're not forcing anything so you can influence others. You're just enforcing the rule of decency so everyone can have their voices heard.

There are 3 things you can do to make the situation lighter.

A - Change the topic of the conversation.
B - Excuse someone you feel like is already very uncomfortable in the situation.
C - Make a joke about how everybody seems tense and how you should all calm down instead.

Action Guide:

1 - Be aware of other people's body language in a group conversation. Sometimes, we can notice if someone is getting uncomfortable or antsy against the other person. We can save this person a lot of pain by either changing the topic, putting more attention to other people, or excusing the person feeling uncomfortable in the conversation.

41

2 - If the conversation starts heating up, try to calm the room by making a light joke of the situation.

20 - Invite People on Dinners

If you like to connect with more people in your industry, then this strategy is a must do! Dinners are usually very intimate and are only done by people who knew each other.

By inviting people to group dinners, you automatically become the connector of the group. You become the person who binds the group together. This gives you lots of social points and it makes you "the man" - someone who cares about each individual who attends the dinner. This also leads to more business opportunities and even life-long friendships.

You don't have to be the one talking all the time. Just by being the moderator, you automatically gain respect and admiration from the people you invited. By being the connector, you become the unofficial leader of this group. And that's as powerful as you can get.

Action Guide:

1 - Invite people with lots of different skills and expertise in different fields.

2 - Come up with a match for each individual who will attend the dinner. If someone has a restaurant, then try to invite a good chef or someone who's good at restaurant marketing. Try to match them by how much value they can give to the other attendees. And then introduce them to each other or place their seat side by side.

3 - If it's a small group, let them talk on the stage for 30 seconds so they can introduce themselves and talk about what they do for a living.

21 - Protect Your Voice

I don't mean this in a metaphysical way. I mean this in the literal sense of the word. Your voice is an instrument that you use for your daily conversations. You use it so you can influence other people.

What if one day, you wake up and you can't speak anymore? That would probably be the worst day of your life. Why? Because you'll feel powerless. It's the only natural communication device that you have that most people can understand.

The point is, you should take care of your voice. Treat it as an asset that you need to look at. An asset that you need to nurture. Protect your voice at all cost because it is a valuable tool that you use in connecting with other people.

Action Guide:

1 - Speak with clarity but avoid shouting.

2 - If you use your voice all day long, try not to speak too much on the next day.

3 - Use a voice spray when you feel your throat getting dry.

4 - Drink water after every hour or so. Avoid caffeine like coffee and tea.

22 - Calm Your Nerves

One of the most important skills that an FBI negotiator needs is learning how to calm his own nerves. If the criminal notice that the negotiator is acting weird and nervous, then the criminal might do something stupid or stop the negotiation.

You are probably not an FBI negotiator but this is still a skill that you should have. Learning to calm your nerves affects how other people communicate with you.

If you come up to a girl and you're sweating and fidgeting, she will notice it and you'll come across as needy and weird. If you're in a business meeting and you start acting weird, then your potential investors might get scared and not invest with you.

Calming your nerves is an important part of good communication because it shows a non-verbal signal that you're in control. It shows that you don't get spook easily. That you're someone who can handle the pressure.

Action Guide:

1 - If you're nervous about something, start breathing in and out for 3 seconds each. Do it 5-10 times and you'll start to immediately notice less nervousness.

2 - Stand up straight with your shoulders back. This shows dominance and the physical act of doing it automatically makes us feel good about ourselves.

3 - Do some stretching exercises. This helps in circulating the blood to your whole body, which then helps in calming your nerves.

23 - Use Insider Language

If you look at every industry, there will always be words that only people in that field will understand. If you want to connect with someone on that market, then you have to know the words that they are speaking.

Let's suppose that you're in the "Internet marketing" world. In that field, you can expect to encounter words like Cost Per Click (CPC), Landing Pages, Squeeze Pages, Clickbait, etc.

These are insider languages that most people probably wouldn't understand. Sure, they're common and basic for the people in the internet marketing space, but they're just random words for normal people outside that market.

Knowing these words mean that you're part of the gang. That you're someone who knows "our language."

One of the hardest parts of traveling abroad is not knowing the language of the locals. Once you already know how to speak their language, you automatically open up a whole new world for you and for them. Suddenly, communication is easier. You get discounts on the food, asking for direction is easy, and you don't get scammed or taken advantage anymore for being a foreigner.

Action Guide:

1 - Learn the insider's language of your market. By simply speaking these words, you become part of the tribe. You're not an outsider anymore. That's because you understand the language and you also use it in your normal conversations.

24 - Make Someone Laugh

It's almost impossible to find a woman who doesn't like a man who makes them laugh. Sure, it's not the only factor on choosing a partner but it's a big part of it. When the looks, money, and lust subside, making someone laugh is something that will never go away.

It's a skill and art at the same time. It's not something that is hard to teach. And it's definitely not a trait that you can have just by taking an online course.

It's developed, trained, and test over the years. And it's something that ironically, the saddest people seem to have.

Whether it's friendship, romantic relationship or business, having the ability to make someone laugh is always a good skill to have on your arsenal.

Action Guide:

So what can you do to get better at being funny?

#1 - The most important aspect of being funny is timing. Timing is knowing when and when not to say the punchline. It's knowing when to blurt something funny and knowing when to shut your mouth.

#2 - Try to write jokes at least once a week. This will help you build your "funny muscle."

#3 - Do not make any insensitive jokes about people dying, gay people, race, or religion.

#4 - Tell stories and exaggerate them to a point that others will wonder whether it's a joke, sarcasm or real.

#5 - Laugh at your own expense. If you joke about yourself, then there's almost 0% chance of someone getting offended by any of it.

25 - Stop Worrying About the Outcome

When we have an important meeting, a date with our dream girl, or a potential life-changing business deal - we tend to be more nervous than usual. We start to do things that may impress other people. We become a little bit more of a people pleaser.

You don't want any of these to happen because people are really good at smelling B.S. They know when you're trying too hard. They know when you're not being yourself. And if they don't know it at the moment, they'll eventually find out if you're lying.

The reason why we do these things is we become suddenly too aware of the potential outcome. We start imagining how awesome things would be. I say we do the opposite. Let's stop worrying about the outcome. Sure, you can do everything in your power to make the outcome positive. But at the end of the day, you don't have any control to what other people would say, feel or do.

Detach yourself from the results and accept the outcome no matter what it is.

Action Guide:

Evaluate your own life and look at some things that you're too attached with. Maybe a coming business deal, a date with your dream guy, or a manager finally signing you to a record deal. No matter what that thing is, start detaching yourself with the possible outcome. Focus on what you can control. Focus on dressing nicely, focus on creating a good presentation, focus on being on time for the meeting...focus on the things that you can do to sway the results in your favor. If you did everything you can, then there's no shame in accepting temporary defeat or failure. Sh*t happens and they happen all the time! You're never going to achieve 100% positive results. You might as well stop worrying about it.

26 - Know When to Shut Your Mouth

Most people think that communication and building social skills are only about speaking. They think that they can make other people like them if they can only say something smart and witty.

But the best communicators also do something that most people do not. They know when to shut their mouth. It seems like a small thing. But it's something that will have a huge effect on how you connect with other people.

Sometimes, we don't notice it but our conversation partner is already dying to say something, or start getting uncomfortable with what you are saying. You have to have the awareness when to continue speaking and when to shut your mouth. This is a skill that you must practice. It's something that will serve you in the long-term. It might even save you from awkward conversations and the potential negative consequences of your words.

Action Guide:

The key to this whole things is this. AWARENESS.

Awareness is looking at different things like:

-The tone of their voice
-Their body language
-Their words
-Their facial reaction to what you're saying

I recommend that you practice your awareness muscle in your next conversation. Look at how the other person reacts to what you say.

Is she sitting in a relaxed manner? Is she smiling on your jokes? Is she fidgeting? Does her tone indicate nervousness, anger or gladness?

These are some of the things that you need to be aware of when you're having a conversation. Knowing when to stop speaking is also as important as knowing what to say.

27 - Give a Social Media Shout-out

One of the easiest ways to gain trust is to give someone a social media shout-out. Basically, you are going to praise them for being good at what they do. In addition, you can also review and recommend their product or services.

By doing these things, you're basically saying how great they are. You are giving them something of value through product or service recommendation.

This is one of the best ways to make someone like you almost instantly. I mean, we can't help it. If someone gives us a shout-out on Facebook and mention how great we are at what we do, we really have no choice but to like that person. That person will be etched in our minds and we will remember him for what he did.

Action Guide:

Post a shout out on Facebook and tag the person on your post.

Here's a short example of what you can do:

So I was just trying to learn how to write a sales page for my product and I found @DakeGriffin (tag him) 6 weeks ago. I studied his free materials on YouTube and I wrote my own sales page 10 days ago based on what he taught in his free videos.

Men, this stuff works! I'm already getting 5 sales per day on a $70 product and I don't even have to deal with any refunds!

Dake is the real deal when it comes to writing sales pages! Thanks again!

If you want to learn more about copywriting, I recommend that you check his YouTube channel @ youtube.com/dake

A simple post like this can take your relationship with Dake to the next level. You can go from a stranger to a potential business partner just by showing your gratitude publicly through Facebook.

You can also do this on Twitter, Instagram or your blog. I do recommend that you start with Facebook because it's easier to see the likes and comments of other people, which also boost the chance of the other person noticing and responding to your post.

28 - Tell Good Stories

Telling good stories is crucial to creating good relationships. Stories are how we make sense of the world around us. Why do you think the bible survived for thousands of years? It isn't just an accident. It's because the bible is full of archetypal human stories.

Stories are how we preserve a memory. Through stories, cultures are built and legends are rediscovered.

Gossip

Although gossip doesn't have a positive connotation nowadays, gossiping is as natural as any skill we humans have. Hundreds of thousand years ago, we gossip so we'll know if there's a threat. We'll gossip so we'll know what is happening in our tribe. Gossiping can be a useful skill to have, but only if we use it the right way.

Story Ark

So how do we tell good stories? How do we become someone whom people likes to listen to?

Whenever I tell stories, to friends, business partners or clients on my business - I follow the simple 3 part act that most stories have.

Act 1 - The Set Up

This is the part where you mention an inciting incident. It is the set up to the story. If you're telling a 30 second story, then this would be as short as three to five sentences.

Act 2 - Confrontation

The confrontation is usually the middle of the story. This is where something bad or exciting happens.

Act 3 - Resolution and Reflection

Act 3 is where the resolution happens. This is the part when the conflict is resolved. This is the part where you tell a fascinating ending to the story.

Example:

Act 1 - The Set Up

"Bro, something weird and a little scary happened to me last night. This girl with all black dress approached me and just blurt my name! I was like "WTF" - that's weird.

Act 2 - Confrontation

"Then she just run out super-fast and I tried to catch her, but then she turned left on a building, and BAM! She was gone. I thought that was weird."

Act 3 - Resolution and Reflection

"The next morning, I saw her in front of my apartment eating a sandwich, she wears black sunglasses and it looks as if she's waiting for someone. Shit dude, I think I have a stalker"

Analysis

Act 1 sets up the whole story. What happened to you that triggered the start of the story? That's your act 1.

Act 2 tells the part where something interesting happened. This is the part where most of the action happens.

Act 3 is where the ending happens and the potential resolution to the story. Act #3 is what happens as a direct result of act #2. It can also be your reflection about what happened and what it means to you.

Action Guide:

1 - Read Maps of Meaning and Hero with a Thousand Faces to learn more about the importance of stories.

2 - Write a short story that you can tell your friends in 1 minute or less. Use the 3-Act method so you will have something fascinating and satisfying to listen to.

29 - Get Them to Say "Yes"

Getting other people to say yes is a skill. And it's a skill that you must master if you want to get the most out of your relationships. No, this isn't about forcing them to do something they don't want to do. It's about asking people to do something that would benefit them as well.

The word "Yes" is a muscle. You must train other people to say yes to you and you must do it often.

Do you want to sell more products? Do you want to offer more services? Do you want to have sexy time with your partner? Do you need someone to do a favor? Then you must learn to ask and they must learn to say yes.

The first thing that you need to do is to be reasonable. You cannot expect other people to say yes to all of your requests. Are you asking for too much? Are you asking too early in the relationship? You cannot ask someone you just met to marry you. You have to court her, make her feel special and get to know her first.

It's the same with training people to say yes. You must ask for smaller things first. Things that won't really make them think twice. It could be as simple as asking them for a dinner or asking them if they've already eaten (even if you knew that they already did). Just get them to say yes in the beginning. This builds the yes muscle and lets you ask for more things in the future. Now, do not abuse other people. Do not ask for anything without giving value first. Make sure that you're also giving something in return to the other person before you ask for lots and lots of yes's.

Action Guide:

1 - Train people to say yes by starting with smaller asks. A simple "did you ate already?" shows concern + getting a yes means adding up the "yes muscle" in their core.

2 - Make sure that you provide value first to other people before you ask for something. If you're a guitar teacher selling your lessons, then you must provide free lessons online before you sell your services. If you're a real estate agent, then you must give people some content first about real estate before sending her your property listings for sale. Provide so much value to other people that they have no choice but to say yes to you more often.

30 - Do Not Interrupt

Do you know people who are interrupters? You'll tell a story about something that happened to you and here he is telling his own story about giant spiders in Amazon. You're here teaching something to your students and some guy would ask stupid questions.

Interrupters are everywhere and we're all annoyed by most of them. They just don't know when to speak and when to shut up. And when you're the one who gets to interrupt, they would look at you badly and they will try to speak louder so he can steal the conversation's attention back to him.

The point is this. Don't be an interrupter.

Seriously, please don't be that guy (or gal).

Unless you have something of value to add to the conversation, then you better just shut your mouth and listen.

Action Guide:

1 - On your next group conversation, learn to shut up and just listen. Count the number of times someone interrupts someone mid-thought. You'll feel good because you're listening, but remember that any other time, just know that you also probably interrupt someone as much as your friend does.

Part 3
Mastering
Your Emotions
and Social Skills

31 - Smile

A smile is as close as we can get to magic when it comes to social skills. People who smile are just more agreeable. We like people who smile because it gives us a sense of comfort.

We associate smiling with feeling good and we immediately get a serotonin boost every time we see someone smile.

Now obviously, there are creepy types of smile. If you're an awkward guy like me, then smiling may be hard for you. Sometimes, I'm too conscious of my teeth and the whole smile itself. So you have to practice and just be comfortable with smiling. A "mini smile" where you don't even show your teeth is perfect for most situations.

Action Guide:

1 - Practice smiling in front of the mirror. Try to do different variations of your smile and then take a picture of each one of them. Choose the best type of smile that you have and then practice that one over and over again in front of the mirror.

2 - Go to your dentist and ask how you can have your best smile. Your dentist should be able to recommend some things that must be fixed with your teeth.

3 - DO THIS: Go to a convenience store and do a "mini-smile" as you ask for something in the cashier. Don't overthink it. Just enough that you're able to bend your lips a little.

32 - Never Say Anything Negative About Anyone in Public

Do you want to make friends or do you want to make enemies? If you're going to trash someone, make sure that you're ready to cut all the relationship (potential relationship) that you have with the other person.

All of us hate backstabbers. We'd rather have someone tell bad sh*t to our face than be talked about behind our backs.

If you're going to criticize someone, try to tell it directly to the other person. Do not mention some passing remarks that may seem harmless. The truth is people gossip all the time - and when people gossip, news spread fast!

I understand that you can never avoid conflicts. But that doesn't mean we cannot lessen it. Instead of making a new enemy, why don't we try to understand where the other party is coming from. Why don't we try to go to the person directly and say our constructive criticism? By doing this, we are actually serving them by helping them get better.

Why make enemies when you can turn people into friends?

Action Guide:

1 - Always think twice about anything that you want to say. When emotions run hot, we say stupid things that may get us in trouble - that we then regret later. Before you post something on Facebook, before you tweet something, before you call and berate someone, before you send that letter - ask yourself, *is this what I really want? Do I want to make new enemies? Do I want to*

suffer from potential loss of this relationship? I guarantee you that 90% of the time, it's just not worth sending that reply.

33 - The Art of an Approach

The focus of the approach is not to close a deal and not to impress on a deeper level. The focus of the approach is to charm someone and give a good first impression. That's it. The goal is to just make ourselves known to the other person. That we exist and we're someone of potential value to that person.

Here are the simple steps that you can use when approaching someone.

A - Recon

The recon is the part where you try to know more about a person before you approach her. Does someone in your circle of friends know her? If she's an influencer, stalk her on Instagram first and see what she likes to share. Anything that can give you context is great information to have.

B - Assess the situation

Next, look at the current situation and assess whether it's the right time to approach or not.

Is she busy? Does she look like she's waiting for someone to approach her? Is she bored? Is she with her friends?

C - Smile and Say Hi

Just literally smile a little, and then say Hi.

D - Say Your Name

Mention your name… "Hi, I'm Andrew" and shake her hands.

E - Ask a Question

Then ask a question immediately while shaking her hands. Questions that may get the conversation going.

Example:

You: "Hi, I'm Andrew, are you friends with Jessie cause I saw you in one of her FB posts last night"

Her: "Yeah, we actually go to the same college."

You: "Awesome, I saw you back there and I thought you were familiar. So what course are you taking?"

And then you ask more questions and just let her talk about herself.

Action Guide:

Practice the 5 step process and approach someone on a bar, a library, a gym or any place you're comfortable with. I challenge you to do it today or tomorrow. This will help increase your confidence when it comes to approaching strangers.

34 - Apologize with Sincerity

A lot of us think that apologizing is a sign of weakness. We think that it means that we're admitting that we're completely wrong and 100% responsible for everything that happened.

But no, apologizing means knowing what you did wrong and learning to forgive yourself at the same time. It's about understanding that even though you're not 100% responsible to what happened, you are taking the higher road so you can fix the problem, gain clarity and have a better relationship with the other person.

When you apologize to someone, make sure that you're sincere. Make sure that you're not just doing it so they would shut up about it already. Apologizing with sincerity means knowing when you messed up. It means that you know what mistakes you made and you now realize how wrong you are with the way you acted about the situation.

Action Guide:

So how do you apologize with sincerity? Just follow these steps:

#1 - Assess the situation. Try to understand what you did wrong and why it was perceived that way.

#2 - Accept that you made a mistake and vow to never let it happen again.

#3 - Forgive yourself for making the mistake. This frees you up and helps lessen the emotional baggage brought by the experience.

#4 - Apologize sincerely by mentioning how the other person might feel right now and mention how you will change things so it won't happen again.

Example:

"Hey Jessie, I know you're mad at me right now and I like to say sorry for what I said last night. I shouldn't have spoken to you that way and I really regret it. I'll do better next time, I promise."

35 - Read Books About How Humans Interact

If you want to learn more about how humans behave, then you have to read the classics. You have to read more books that are a little more philosophical in nature. Why? Because they can serve as the foundation of how you act around people. They will serve as the foundation on how you communicate with people so you can get what you want.

Books are powerful because, on most books, you're getting years of research and experience by the author for as low as $2.99. Invest in your education and continue to learn every single day.

Action Guide:

Order these books on Amazon and read them as soon as you can. They are the most powerful books I read when it comes to understanding how and why people act the way they act.

Influence by Robert Cialdini

48 laws of Power by Robert Greene

Laws of Human Nature by Robert Greene

How to Win Friends and Influence People by Dale Carnegie

The Charisma Myth by Olivia Fox

The Speed of Trust by Stephen Covey

36 - Join a Social Skills Support Group

Social skills improvement groups are everywhere. They are great because you'll get to share your struggles and you'll get to listen to other people's issues. Either way, you'll learn how to deal with your social skills problems and you'll improve faster than you're expecting. Learning from other people is a great way to retain knowledge. The more you communicate with other people, the more you are able to practice what you learn. Having a support group who understands your struggle makes it a little easier to fight through it.

Action Guide:

1 - I recommend that you find one first locally. Search the net for the nearest groups that you can find. Most will be free and some will have paid but cheap admission fees.

Search for things like:

"Social skills/social support group name of your town"
"Social skills/social support group name of your city"

"Introvert support group name of your town"
"Introvert support group name of your city"

2 - I also recommend the website meetup.com. You can search for the topic of the problem and then choose the nearest city/town available.

3 - Talk to a therapist if your social skill problems are already too deep and need a little more focused help.

37 - Attend a Toastmasters Meeting

I always thought that Toastmasters is just a group full of smug people - talking about some random stuff to impress and stroke each other's ego. I didn't know that I was the fool! I didn't realize that there are so many benefits of joining a Toastmasters group. You just need to find a group where it's tight-knit and a group where they really care about each other.

If you want to improve your social skills - whether it's public speaking, conversations and even digital communications - then a Toastmasters meetup is a must try.

You will probably have to try different Toastmaster chapters in the beginning, but once you found that group of people who really care about each other - you will start to realize how important that group is to you not only professionally, but also personally speaking.

Action Guide:

1 - Search for Toastmasters meeting near your area.

http://www.toastmasters.org/Find-a-Club

2 - Be open to the idea of sucking at speaking in front of people. Be open to the idea of making mistakes. Be open to the idea of not being perfect! No one is expecting you to be! One thing I assure you is the majority of people there are rooting for you!

3 - Ask lots and lots of questions to the people who have been there for a while now. People who know what's it like to be a

beginner. People who understand the feeling of not being able to speak in front of other people.

4 - Be consistent and regularly attend meetings.

5 - Get yourself out there and be vulnerable. It shows strength and humility at the same time.

38 - Ditch Your Negative Thoughts Fast!

Whenever we're about to approach someone, talk to someone important or ask for something - we tend to think about the negative things that will happen.

We can't help it. We don't want to disappoint ourselves so we lower our expectations and we let the negative thoughts cloud our judgment and action instead.

This is dangerous because other people can see and feel when you're not acting right. Other people know when something's "just not right." Your negative thoughts affect how you act and how you act affects how other people feel your energy.

Action Guide:

1 - Practice your awareness of negative thoughts. Whenever a negative thought pops out in your mind, immediately wipe it off, theoretically speaking. Imagine as if you're putting a fan in front of a bubble and then letting that negative bubble fly off as far as you can imagine.

2 - Replace that negative thought with something positive. When you start thinking about how you're going to get rejected, imagine the complete opposite instead. Imagine how well the conversation is going to be. Imagine how agreeable you will find the other person to be. How you really feel will project itself in the way you act, thus making a conversation beneficial for both of you.

39 - Be Assertive But Not Aggressive

First, I want to make it clear that being assertive is different from being annoying, clingy and aggressive.

Being assertive means taking responsibility to start something. Is your conversation partner shy and reserved? Then start the conversation and ask something interesting. Do you feel like a group of students wants to approach you and ask something important? Go ahead, let them know that you're there if they have any questions.

Assertive people, I believe, are the ones who get what they want. They are the ones who achieve great things because they are willing to put themselves out there. They're willing to get rejected, they're willing to get humiliated - because they know that being assertive and going for the things that they want is worth the risk.

Action Guide:

HOW TO PRACTICE ASSERTIVENESS

1 - Stop being a fly in the wall. Sometimes, we get too passive and we never go for something that we really want.

2 - Start a conversation with someone. Introduce a topic instead of letting them dictate what you guys are going to talk about.

In your next conversation, think of a topic that your friend finds interesting. Try to lead her instead of her leading you. Ask open-ended questions, the ones that starts with HOW and WHY.

40 - Don't Be "That Guy"

I'm sure you already experienced this. You have some friends or colleagues that you refer to as "that guy."

"That Guy" can mean a lot of things. But usually, it doesn't have a positive connotation.

"That Guy" could mean that you're that annoying dude who always talks to everyone in the office even on busy hours. You're that guy who acts creepy around girls. Your that guy who always brags about what he did last weekend. Your that guy who always annoy other people.

In most offices, there's always seem to be one person who's "that guy." (by the way, this also applies to women as well)

If you can't find who "that guy" is, then start looking at your own behavior cause you might be "that guy."

Action Guide:

1 - Start evaluating your own behavior. Do you do some things that you might find normal, but in reality, it could be something that already bothers other people?

I used to be that guy who's always talking to friends from different office departments. There's nothing wrong with that per se, but I tend to do it during office hours when everyone is busy.

2 - Make sure that you're not "that guy"

41 - Accept Criticism with an Open Mind

I used to get butthurt by every criticism I received during my early 20's. I always thought that I was on the right. I always thought that my way is the right way.

Looking back, I realize how big of a smart-ass as I was back then. During those times, I would take it personally every time someone criticizes me. Instead of looking at what I did wrong, I would always find a way to justify my actions. I never listen to most of what my boss would say. It all goes through my right ear and goes out to the left - fast!

If I can go back to those times, I would give myself a big slap in the face so I would sober up and see what's really going on.

How about you? Are you also acting this way when it comes to your friends, family, boss, employees, etc.?

Do you always think that your way is the right way? Do you accept criticisms or do you always find a way to justify the wrong things that you do?

Action Guide:

Learn to accept criticisms without bitterness. If the one giving it is a trusted friend, family member or co-worker, then just know that what they're saying is most likely going to help you get better. Be on the watch out for your next mistake/failure - you are likely to get some criticism out of it. The important part is to take that criticism and accept that you made a mistake. Then vow to never make the same mistake again.

42 - Be Open to Implementing Their Suggestions

There's a difference between accepting criticism and implementing the solution. Accepting criticism is a good first step. Acknowledging that you're wrong is a powerful agent of change. But what do you do next so it doesn't have to happen again?

The next part is the implementation. Once you realize your mistake, ask for something that you can do so you can get a better results next time. Ask for constructive criticism. Be assertive and ask for specific things you can apply.

Let's say that you didn't submit a blog content that your boss asked for. You know that you're super busy and you can't submit it by Friday but you never told him about it. Ask him what you can do next and what solution you guys may do so it'll never have to happen again.

Action Guide:

It's not enough to accept criticism. It's also important that you use the constructive criticism to get better. Use the criticism and actually do something about the problem. The purpose of the criticism is not to make you feel bad. The purpose of the criticism is not to berate you or make you feel useless for making a mistake. No. The purpose of criticism is to make you understand the wrong thing that you did so you never have to make the same mistake again.

Ask yourself, how can you apply this kind of mindset In your own work or relationships? Think of some of the things that you should get better at and then start finding solutions for those problems.

43 - Know the Unspoken Rules of Communication Platforms

Improving your social skills is a never-ending task. It's something that is impossible to master. Human behavior is not likely to change but we still have to keep up with the technological progress that affects how we make conversations.

You must continually learn how to communicate on different types of platforms. You must know the do's and don'ts for every platform that we use.

Face to face, video calls, audio calls, e-mails, Facebook comments, tweets, etc.

Now, you don't have to master all of them. But society expects you to know the unspoken rules of communicating using these platforms.

For example, on Twitter, you should be very careful in replying to some ridiculous tweets. Why? Because a lot of tweets that you will see nowadays are sarcastic ones. If you get offended easily, then you shouldn't be there in the first place. Sarcasm is a language that a lot of people use on Twitter. So you need to accept that and you also need to know who's the one tweeting. Is he constantly tweeting sarcastic tweets? Then do not engage an act of hostility or you will be twitter's laughing stock.

Action Guide:

Most platforms will have some kind of unspoken rule like the one in my example. So continue to learn and make sure that you're not being oblivious to the rules of the platform you are using.

44 - Respecting Other People's Time

Some people just don't know how to value other people's time. They'll just barge in and call for an "emergency meeting" that should've been scheduled days ago.

If you know how to respect other people's time. Then they will reciprocate this action and they will respect yours as well. If not, at least you can train them to do so.

What does respecting other people's time mean?

It means not interrupting when they're saying something important. It means not trying to steal their thunder. It means not asking for emergency meetings every day. It means asking for something in a polite manner.

If you need someone to photocopy a set of papers for you, try not to ask for it during peak hours. If you do that, then they might miss their own work deadlines. Asking politely means trying not to be too bossy even though you clearly have a higher position than the other person.

Action Guide:

1 - Always be considerate when it comes to asking for other people's time. All of us are busy and trying our best to fulfil the tasks that we are supposed to do. You asking for their time means you're getting something they can never get back.

2 - Ask respectfully. Use words like "kindly and please."

E.g.

"Hey Joe, kindly go to my office at 4pm later as I need to talk to you about project X."

"Hi Sarah, this is gonna be quick and I need 3 minutes of your time. Can you please go to my office now? Thanks."

Part 4
Social Skills Precision

45 - Know Your Signature Looks

Your signature looks can act as your "identifier." Think Barney Stinson in How I Met Your Mother. He always wears suits and he's defined as someone as the guy who wears suits. Now, you don't want to be overly defined by what you wear. But if you are new to the organization, try to create a wardrobe that will serve as your "costume" for work.

Costume in a sense that whenever they see someone wearing that type of dress, you're the first one that they will remember.

You can wear navy blue suits or dark grey suits if you're a man, and go for dresses or professional dresses if you're a woman.

This applies not only in the office setting but also in other places. Create your signature look and people will recognize you faster and easier. The key here is to build your wardrobe and make it stand out a little. By doing this, you be easily remembered by strangers, potential business partners, investors, customers, and clients.

Action Guide:

1 - Watch "how to build your professional wardrobe for men/for women" on YouTube.

2 - Invest in the basics that you need like suits, dresses, shoes, and pants. People will always judge a book by its cover. It's the same with your appearance. The more professional you are to look at, the more business you will get.

Most people's social media and real-life persona are so vastly different that we're likely to not recognize some of them we if we see them in real life.

On Instagram, they look perfect. Tan lines, no scars, pretty face, red lips, perfect eyebrows, etc. They appear rich, successful and even famous...

But when you see them in real life, you'll realize that they're just like everybody else. Normal.

Look, I want you to dress well and present yourself as a neat looking person. I'm not discouraging people to look ugly online. No. I only want people to be their true selves. If they have acne scars, then don't be afraid to show it on the picture. No need to edit your face for 2 hours just so you can look pretty. If you have belly fat, then no need to find the perfect angle for an hour just so you'll have an amazing looking body on your summer pic.

Action Guide:

My advice is simple. Be true to yourself. While everybody else is trying to impress other people just so they can get more than 100 likes on their posts, go out there and YOU JUST BE YOU. That's the best things you can do. Match your online persona with who you really are in real life - and other people will start to recognize who you really are. Make them more interested in your values, knowledge, and character instead of your physical appearance.

47 - Don't Brag

Nobody likes a bragger.

It doesn't matter if you're the richest person in the club. Sure, you might get girls or guys circling you like a vulture waiting for his meal to die, but at the end of the day - a bragger almost always ends up lonely, unfulfilled and alone.

Do not brag about your fast cars, houses, extremely expensive vacations and how much you earn last month. Other people may get inspired but most will only see the "result." They will never see the work that you did (or your parents lol) for you to have all these things.

Focus on the process instead. Share your struggles, share the things that you're learning along on your journey.

Connecting with people is easier if you're genuinely interested in helping them. If you only post about your vacations and how good your life is, most people will just get turned off by you. Most people will start to hate what you have instead of being inspired by it.

Action Guide:

1 - Never brag about the material things that you have (how much you earn, your cars, your house). Seriously, nobody likes a bragger.

2 - Feel free to brag about your friends, clients, and customers success stories. If you are going to brag, then go brag about other people.

48 - Give Other People Credit

Always, always, always give credit where credit is due.

If a co-worker did something awesome, then try to let other people know about it. If your staff did most of the work and you get the award for being a good leader, then make sure that you share the glory to your team - in your thank you speech, in a company memo/greetings, or through face to face.

The more credit you give to other people, the more you become a person they like and respect.

You're not just there to grab all the credits. You're a person who's willing to share the praise, the rewards, and the benefits.

Action Guide:

Practice giving credit to other people.

If you got praised for raising your child well, then give credit to your wife and let them know about the awesome things she taught your kids.

If your team got an award for the best sales team, then give a part of your personal bonus to your staff or treat them for dinner. Do anything that would make them feel appreciated.

Give credit where credit is due.

49 - Take Advantage of the Mirror Neurons

Mirror neurons are chemicals in our brain that gives us the ability to learn, mimic or copy. It's an essential part of growing up, adapting and learning how to communicate well.

Mirror neurons also help us mimic body language, facial expressions, and emotions.

If you know how to maximize your mirror neurons, you'll be able to understand others better and be able to connect almost effortlessly.

Imagine knowing how someone feels just by looking at his face. Imagine being able to identify the body language that your conversation partner is expressing. Understanding how mirror neurons works will help you in being able to relate more and connect on a deeper level.

So how do you actually use it? Well, here's the tricky part - there's no specific thing that you can do to "use it." Your mirror neurons are just there naturally. You can only cultivate it by practicing awareness. You can only use it by having a watchful eye.

Action Guide:

1 - Practice awareness when it comes to other people's facial expressions and body language. On your next conversation, be aware of how someone uses their facial expression whenever they are speaking. If she's talking about something scary, watch if her face wrinkles a little and look at her eyes at the same time - you will notice that she has a more intense look than normal. Another

thing to look at is her body language. Is she more guarded? Hunch forward? Or does she sit with her shoulders back?

Hunching forward means she's really into it and she's really serious about what she's talking about. Having her shoulders back means she's confident and not afraid of any possible danger.

50 - Culture Awareness - Respect and Politeness

Every culture has different practices, and for some of these manners, other people may find them weird. Italians like to kiss cheek to cheek. Filipinos hold an elder's hand and let their forehead touch the knuckles of their grandparent's hand. Westerners prefer handshake over hugging -, especially for males.

Whatever these manners or practices are, we should learn to respect each other's culture and try not to make any snide comment about how others conduct their business.

Respect is the name of the game. As long as they're not hurting anybody, then what they do and follow in their culture is none of your business. Instead, you should try to understand what they're doing and why they're doing it. Most of the time, there's some historical significance in why they do what they do.

Action Guide:

1 - Research about different cultures from different races. A few minutes of reading Wikipedia will give you a better understanding of other people's culture.

I recommend that you start with the Maoris culture, especially the dance that they do - find out what it means to them and search for the historical significance of the dance.

51 - Use the Right Voice Tone

Where I'm from, we tend to speak louder and we have this reputation as the province of the brave. That is why a lot of people get culture shocked every time they go to our province. They think that people are fighting and being at each other's throat. I laughed at it at first because these all seem normal to me. But when I started working in a big city, I realized that the tone of our voice affects how others look at us.

A higher and faster tone usually means that we're scared or nervous about something. A lower and slower tone means we are relaxed and we're comfortable about a certain subject.

A louder tone means we're angry or we want something heard clearly. And a quiet tone means we don't want others to hear what we are saying - it's likely that we're ashamed, in denial or uncomfortable with what we're saying.

Action Guide:

Use the tone of your voice wisely. In your conversations, you should use a variety of tone or else, other people would find that conversation monotonous and boring. If you're telling a scary story, then lower your voice and speak more quietly. If you're talking about something exciting, then pitch your voice on a higher tone and speak a little bit faster than usual. Your voice tone affects how others feel about what you're saying. You must match the context of the story to the tone of your voice.

52 - Give Someone a Gift

Giving a gift is a significant act of gratefulness. It is also a congratulatory act that most people would appreciate.

Now, giving a gift should be an act that you do without expecting something in return. The Law of Reciprocity is always at work and people will always want to give something in return - but you have to be genuine and you have to expect nothing from the other party.

Whether it's your business partner, employees, staff, students and family members - giving a gift will always bring a spark of joy in whoever you give it to.

Giving someone a gift also gives a higher chance of connecting with someone you want to do business with. When you give gifts, you stand out. People remember you and people appreciate your gesture.

Action Guide:

Use the power of gift giving to increase your chances of closing business deals or connecting with someone.

A gift is powerful but you shouldn't use it to take advantage of someone's emotion. Treat it as a tool that you can use to connect with other people, but do not abuse its power and never expect something in return.

The best gifts I found are watches, electronic devices, and personalized items like mugs & caps.

53 - Eye Contact is Gold

You've already heard this in hundreds of self-help books. Eye contact is a crucial aspect of connecting with other people. It's something that you need to do in order to gain someone's trust.

Someone not looking at the eye of the person speaking is probably not interested in what he has to say. He might also be ashamed of something and it also shows that he's uncomfortable with what they are talking about.

We live in a world where everybody likes to just stay at home and talk to no one. So whenever you get the chance to hang out with your friends, go put down the phone and look at them instead. Your phone should be turned upside down or be in your pocket so it won't disturb your conversation.

Action Guide:

1 - Look at the other person's eye at least 50% of the time.

2 - Do not look at your feet. This shows non-interest and it gives the message that you don't care about what the other person is saying.

3 - Do not look up to the sky as if you're wondering when your next vacation will be. This is another act that shows that you're not interested in what the other person has to say.

4 - In a group setting, always look at the person who is speaking.

54 - Be Knowledgeable About Current Events

Sometimes, people just ran out of things to talk about. This may turn a supposed great conversation into a bad one.

Ever had those awkward pauses where literally no one is speaking. Those gaps are a little uncomfortable and it's something that kills the mood and flow of a conversation.

What I recommend is that you become aware of what is currently happening to the world. Just be knowledgeable about current news event so you have something to talk about. Now, be a little careful here and try not to talk about politics if possible. Nothing kills a vibe more than a group of close friends arguing about who's right and who's wrong about politics. Politics is a dirty business and I usually would avoid talking about it - because, to me, it's just not worth it.

Action Guide:

Be aware of the current news events and familiarize yourself with what is happening to the world. I would avoid watching the news on TV. Instead, I will spend a few minutes looking at Google News. Don't spend any more than 15 minutes a day. Just being aware of something is good enough since most news sites talk about the same thing over a period of 1-2 weeks.

55 - Master Small Talk

"How's the weather"

"How's your Euro trip?"

"Men, this rain sucks right?"

"Have you seen the ending of Game of Thrones? It's crazy right?"

These small talks may not be interesting. They may not make a productive conversation. But they will serve as the gateway for a deeper conversation. It's hard to talk about the hard stuff in the beginning. You cannot just talk about the world's problems and immediately go into more complex topics. You have to start with something relatively easy.

That's where small talk comes in. Small talks serve as the appetizer to your main course. Its function is to make the conversation start on a comfortable level. You wouldn't ask someone you just met to marry you. That would be insane. You start with introducing yourself. You ask for more things about her. Then you go a little deeper and ask more personal stuff on the 8th date.

Small talk is powerful, as long as you let it do its job.

Action Guide:

1 - Start your conversation with small talk. Be comfortable in talking about the weather, sports, or entertainment.

56 - Say "Thank You" More Often

How easy is it to say these words? Seriously, why aren't we saying this more? Why are we always in a hurry? Why are we so inconsiderate of other people's small act of kindness? Just say thank you whenever you can...

Did someone open the door for you? Say thank you.

Someone said that your suit looks good on you? Say thank you.

Someone gave you a bottle of water because she noticed how tired you are? Say thank you.

Someone let you borrow his phone so you can call your wife? Say thank you.

Action Guide:

1 - Make it a mission to say the word "thank you" today. Any little thing that others do for you, say thanks and be genuinely grateful for that small act of kindness.

2 - Practice saying "thank you" 100 times in the mirror. Condition your brain to say these 2 words all the time and you'll have a more positive outlook in life. Also, this will make other people feel good about themselves while also attaching that feeling of happiness through your words. So the next time they see you, they'll immediately feel warm and fuzzy inside. They won't notice it consciously but they will start to like you more and treat you better than everybody else.

57 - Find Common Grounds

The best way to connect with someone is to find your common grounds. These are things that you do, hobbies that you have and your entertainment preferences.

By having something in common to talk about, you immediately lessen the chance of having awkward pauses. By talking about the same interest, both of you can say a lot of things and voice your opinion freely.

Here are some of the things that you may find in common with other people:

Sports
What they watch on tv
What music they like
What school did they go to

Talking about these things may open up the conversation into something deeper. Something more interesting and something that will benefit both of you. The conversation may start with Game of Thrones and may end up a potential business deal. Don't be afraid to talk about something "less important," they usually open up possibilities for better relationships and a deeper understanding of each other.

Action Guide:

If you're talking to someone you want to build a deeper relationship with, then the best things to talk about are your hobbies and your interests in life. Start with what she is passionate about and let her talk about it as much as she can.

58 - Be Precise in Your Speech

What does being precise in your speech mean? Does it mean that you have to always say the right thing? Does it mean that you have to have perfect grammar? Well, no.

Being precise in your speech means cutting out unnecessary parts of your story. Being precise in your speech means not going back and forth when you're trying to make a point.

We all have that friend who needs to tell the whole history of Alexander the Great before he tells that he died from a mysterious disease.

Most of the time, there will be parts of your story that doesn't need to be mentioned. If it doesn't serve any purpose to what you're saying, then there's no need to mention it.

Action Guide:

The next time you tell a story, make sure that you cut the fat and stop mentioning the unnecessary details. The unnecessary details are the supposed supporting details that will make the ending more better. If your point is to tell how Alexander the Great died from a mysterious disease, then him playing Pollo probably doesn't have to be in your story.

Part 5
Self-Esteem, Negotiation and Honesty

59 - Be Patient

There are times when you will be tested. There are times when there will be some super annoying person that just won't stop talking about stuff you don't care about.

This is when you need patience the most.

It's easy to say that you're patient when a conversation is light and comfortable. But what if the topic is making you uncomfortable? What if the other person disagrees with your views? What if what he is saying go against what you believe in? Do you act irrationally and starts spewing nonsense? Or do you try to understand the other person?

This is what's wrong with our society today.

People from the left thinks that people who want to have a wall created are racist. Then people from the right thinks that all leftist are snowflakes who easily get offended by everything. Why don't we try to create a conversation?

Look, you are not going to change somebody's mind by insulting him. This is where patience comes in. Us willing to have a discussion is a sign of patience and character - and that's what we should strive for.

Action Guide:

1 - Give other people the benefit of the doubt. Be patient in your conversations and never assume anything unless stated otherwise.

2 - Be open to having a discussion with those people who disagree with you.

60 - Be Polite

Are you one of those guys or gals who thinks that they're better than everybody? Do you try hard to be the alpha? Do you think, you being smug makes you more likeable and respected?

Well, you got it wrong buddy.

People generally like people who are very polite and respectful.

People who still say, sir or mam. People who respect the elders. People who don't interrupt. People who still respect the culture where they come from. People who know that the most important thing a man can have is the strength of his character.

One of those enduring characters is politeness.

Action Guide:

Do one thing today that will show politeness and respect to a stranger. An act of politeness doesn't have to be something of a grand gesture. Shake somebody's hand. Look people in the eye when they are talking. Listen to a friend genuinely.

A small act of politeness goes a long way for sure.

61 - Ask Yourself, "Do I Really Need to Say This?"

There are a lot of times when we would speak up about something even when nobody really asks for our opinion. We are a generation of people who think that we should all have *a take* on something. You have to have a take about banning guns. You have to have a take about the Kardashians. You have to have a take about basketball. You have to have a take about Russia.

Seriously, this is so effin' dumb. If you haven't taken the time to actually know the details of a certain issue, then do you really have to have a take on it?

Look, you can research, study and learn more about a certain topic - that's when you are given a voice. Not when you don't know sh*t about anything.

Action Guide:

1 - The next time you voice your opinion, ask yourself this question first.

Do I Really Need to Say This?

Are you adding some kind of value to the conversation? Is what you have to say important enough to warrant a few minutes of back and forth conversations? Are you only saying it because you want to sound smart?

Be honest with your answers here. After all, nobody really likes a *know it all.*

62 - Do Not Be a Bully

A lot of people are bullies.

In their mind, if they can only make other people afraid of them, then they can finally become the alpha. And if they're the alpha, then everyone would just naturally come close to them.

The truth is you don't need to be a bully to gain someone's respect. You don't have to be a bully to show "who's boss."

You probably don't think that you're a bully. So you have to look at everything you're doing - and think twice about it. Are you always trying to make your cashier move faster? Are you always cutting lines on trains and restaurants? These are just some of the things that we do to bully other people. Bullying isn't just about the usual school bullying. It's about trying to step on other people's feet.

So what can you do about it?

Focus on gaining respect. On gaining admiration for the good things you are doing. Focus on giving value to other people. Focus on solving their problems.

If you do these things, then connecting with someone is easy. If you know how to project your best self, and if you do it genuinely, then you will gain respect, love, and admiration.

No question about it.

Action Guide:

Do not (or stop) bullying people just so they will do something for you. Stop controlling other people through fear. Instead, focus on gaining their respect.

By doing this, you can build a reputation based on things that actually matter - being a good person, being a trusted friend and building something good for other people.

63 - Know Your Stuff

Do you want to gain instant respect from your peers? Do you want to be a trusted advisor? Do you want to become someone who everybody loves and respect? Do you want to become someone other people like to talk to?

Then you have to know your stuff.

You see, people always talk a big game. Yet they barely produce anything that resembles what they've been preaching.

If you want people to respect your position, then you have to know your own stuff.

Or as the Rated R version of this would say…

"Know Your Sh*t"

Action Guide:

1 - Commit to improving your skill set this year.

2 - Look at the things that you can do every day so you can learn more about your expertise/market.

Things like taking a course, attending a seminar, practicing every day, hiring a coach, joining an apprenticeship, etc.

64 - Know How to Resolve a Conflict

Knowing how to resolve a conflict means being the moderator between 2 parties, even if one of those party is you. The moderator knows how to create a conversation. He understands that nothing is going to get resolved unless both of them sit down and talk about their differences.

Once you have 2 people willing to listen to each other, you have to make sure that you enforce the rule and make it a civil and respectful discussion. This is not going to be a debate. This is going to be about the truth. The more honest both the parties are, the easier the conflict will be solved.

Action Guide:

Conflict Resolution 101

1 - Find out what happened. What is it you or 2 parties are arguing about.

2 - Create a safe space for both of you. That means each will be given an ample amount of time to mention their sides of the story.

3 - Be the first to admit any wrong thing that you did. Take some of the blame especially if you know in yourself that it's warranted. By this time, the other person may also admit some of the blame for himself.

4 - Mention what you could've done better.

5 - Apologize to each other and promise to learn from this event/ your mistake.

65 - Be Honest ... And Be Kind

Tell the truth as much as possible. Why? Because not telling the truth almost always has some kind of long-term repercussion. Lying so you wouldn't hurt someone's feeling may be a good idea now. But in the long-term, you're just hurting that other person because you're too afraid and feel uncomfortable about saying the truth.

Now, there's always a better way to tell a hard truth.

You can say it in a kind and respectful manner.

If one of your friends ask if you can loan him money for gambling, then be honest and tell him something like this:

"Yes, I do have money but I don't think I should lend it to you. Look, brother, I'm a little concerned about you. You've been spending too much money on playing lately and you might get yourself into too much debt"

Saying this may make you uncomfortable. This may even piss off your friend. You might even get judged because you have all this money and you don't want to lend some for a friend.

That's the uncomfortable truth that you have to endure. But in the long term, it's all going to be worth it because you're actually helping someone by being honest now - by telling your truth - now.

Action Guide:

1 - Stop lying to your friends, family members, business partners and anyone you communicate with.

2 - Identify a part of your life where you constantly lie about.

Do you keep telling your wife that she's not fat, even though she's already 100 lbs overweight?

Are you too afraid to tell someone to change her habit of being late?

Telling the truth requires courage and even short term sacrifice. What you can do best is to be kind in the manner that you tell the truth. If it's painful to say, then don't say it in a direct manner.

For example:

Instead of saying...

"Yes, you got fat"

Then you can do this instead...

Invite your wife to a serious conversation.

Tell her that you love her no matter what and let her know that you are concern about her health. If you are genuine and if you really love each other, she will understand where you are coming from.

66 - Decide Fast!

People think that most decisions is binary. That it's either a yes or a no.

Let's suppose that you are inviting someone to invest in your new start-up. You made your pitch, you did your best and you're just waiting for the decision.

The only answer you can expect is a yes or a no. But what if he's taking too much time to decide? What if 2 months have passed and you still haven't heard a solid commitment from him? That's the gap that you want to avoid. You want to be able to make decisions fast.

If you are in the investor's shoes, then you need to realize that indecisions are already costing you money, time, freedom, and peace of mind. You being indecisive is already affecting other people around you. Being indecisive means other people may have already gotten your spot.

Serious players also hate indecisive people. They want someone who can take control. They want someone who can make tough decisions fast.

Remember this, you will never be able to play in the big leagues in terms of sports, business, and entertainment if you are not willing to make quick decisions.

Action Guide:

1 - This will be an unusual action guide but I suggest that you still do it.

Go play arcade games that forces you to make snap decisions. I like arcade games because most of them are zero-sum games. They force your brain to decide on whether to go right or go left. Up or down. Walk or run. Jump or duck.

You get hit by a turtle, you're dead (Mario Bros). You get close to a ghost, then you get eaten and you're dead (Pacman).

2 - I also recommend that you read Malcolm Gladwell's book Blink: The Power of Thinking Without Thinking.

67 - Learn to Say No

Most people think that they have to say yes to everything someone asks for just so they would like them. We think that we have to always be available. We make ourselves the "Yes Man (or woman). After all, those who say yes to things always gets the glory right? Wrong.

The truth is, we have to be as careful as to what we say no to as to what we say yes to.

We saying no to things means we are prioritizing our time. Saying no to one opportunity also opens up better opportunities for us.

This might be something hard to do in the beginning. But once you become comfortable with rejecting people, then it'll get easier. And in the long term, you'll be able to have better relationships, become more productive, earn money and be happier.

Action Guide:

1 - Practice say NO multiple times in the mirror.

2 - The next time someone asks you for something (especially if it's something not too important). Just say no. You don't have to explain your reasons. Just say no and move on.

68 - Nod

Want it to look like you're listening? Nod.
Want it to look like you're interested in what the other party has to say? Nod.
Want it to look like you're approving of something? Nod.

1 word. 1 action. Yet too powerful not to use.

Now, make sure that you're nodding because you actually care. Make sure that you're nodding because you're actually giving approval. Make sure that you're nodding because you're actually interested.

Faking your nod may lead to some misunderstanding later.

Action Guide:

1 - Nod to show other people your approval or interest.

2 - Don't fake your nod because it will come back to bite your ass in the near future.

69 - Know What They Want and Need

Everybody want or need something from other people. It doesn't matter who you are. You will always have to get something from someone - and that doesn't have to be a negative thing.

Knowing what other people want and need is the first step in creating a relationship with them. Let's say that you're a life insurance salesman. What do people need that you have? Well, you have the ability to help them be insured, have potential money that they can use in case of medical emergencies or death.

In that context, you now know what you can offer that others may find valuable. Your conversations are going to be about making them realize how important your product and service is.

So you got to have context on your conversations. You have to know their goals, wants, needs and aspiration so you'll know exactly what you can talk about.

Action Guide:

In your professional conversations, always come from a place of help. What can you give or offer that they may find valuable? Find what they want and give a solution to their problem.

If you want to practice solving problems, you can go to Twitter and search for words like:

"I wish there was"

"This sucks"
"I hope there is"
"Is there a solution for"

These are the words that signals the problem.
By searching for these, you'll know what problems people want to solve. This exercise will give you an awareness of the hundreds of problems that you can solve for other people.

70 - Prepare to Negotiate

Not every deal will go according to what you want. Sometimes, there would be problems with the numbers. Sometimes, the other party would want to get something more out of you.

Learning to properly negotiate can help you maximize your chance of closing a good deal.

Now, there are lots of factors that affects a deal. I can't possibly discuss everything here right now. However, I'm going to give you my top 5 factors that affects a deal.

#1 - Trust

Before anything else, the other person must trust you even before you sell them the idea. Trust is something built on a relationship. How long have you known each other? Have you provided the other person any value in the past?

#2 - Like

Does your personality match? Do you guys like the same things? The hardest deals to close are the ones where both parties hate each other.

#3 - Status

Status comes from being someone who's known in your industry. Celebrities like Brad Pitt and Angelina Jolie has 10/10 status. Now, we don't have to be a celebrity to gain status. In fact, status can be manufactured - through PR, podcast, Facebook and YouTube Videos, testimonials, and books. If you have any of these things, then people naturally see you on a higher status inside your industry.

#4 - Clash of Interest

Not all deals can be win-win, but the closer you get it to a 50-50 agreement, the better. You have to give them a reasonable agreement for both of your interest. Each one of you probably wants to make money - but you have to make the other party understand that if you don't make any money, then he won't either.

#5 - Price

This isn't the most important but it's still part of the game. You have to set the right price for a client or vice versa. The right price means a client should be getting more or equal value than what he paid for.

Action Guide:

Practice your negotiation skills by starting on smaller deals. Heck, you can even start by haggling with someone on your local market. This is a good first practice because there's really nothing at risk here. You're not there to save millions. You're just there to buy something that'll cost you no more than $20.

71 - Learn the Right Way of Greeting People

Greeting people is a fundamental part of improving your social skills.

A conversation usually starts with a greeting and the more genuine you are, the easier the conversation will be.

A greeting is simple, right?

Just say "Hi Anne" and you're done???

What I found is it is better to start a conversation by asking a question or by giving them a compliment.

Example:

"Hi Anne, nice shoes"

"Hi Anne, I haven't seen you in a while, what are you up to these days?"

"Hi Anne, you're looking good, do you go to the gym every day?"

Action Guide:

Practice saying Hi to a friend or a colleague and then find something to complement immediately.

72 - Don't Be "Salty"

You'll be amazed at how many salty people are out there. It doesn't matter if you're a millennial, generation X Y Z or whatever - there will always be salty people around you. Heck, it could be you.

Salty people are the ones who can't move on from an insult. Salty people are the ones who are easily offended by everything.

Some white girl wears a taco during Halloween and the salty people loses their mind. A black kid wears a cowboy hat and that salty white dude starts ranting on his blog.

What a stupid way to live.

Trust me, nobody likes a salty guy or gal. Your friends may even pretend to like you - but they probably even talk shit about you behind your back.

Action Guide:

1 - Stop hanging out with salty people.

2 - Look at yourself and honestly asses if you are the "salty guy/gal" in the group.

3 - Commit to changing your attitude by being more open to failures and criticisms.

73 - Take Responsibility

This is, I believe the ultimate social skill. Why? Because it has nothing to do with other people. It's something that you create within. No outside factor can affect your choice of taking responsibility. People like and trust someone who knows how to accept responsibility. People like someone who knows how to take the blame. People like someone who doesn't blame other people for his misery.

It's no accident why the archetypal hero that the modern civilization have is Jesus. Jesus made the ultimate sacrifice for all mankind. Now, I'm not asking you to believe in Christianity or any religion for that matter. I just want you to look at the significance of what Jesus stands for.

Action Guide:

1 - Stop blaming other people for your misery.

2 - Start taking responsibility. What can you do to make your life better? What are the things that you need to change in order to build a better life?

3 - Tattoo the thought below in your mind. This is deep but worth the time to actually think about.

"Between stimulus and response, there is a space. In that space is our power to choose our response. In our response lies our growth and our freedom." —Viktor E. Frankl

4 - Read Man's Search for Meaning by Viktor E. Frankl.

74 - Generate Solutions

Nobody likes to talk to a problem sharer. These are the type of people who always gossip. These are the type of people who always seem to talk about other people, their problems, how bad everything is, and pretty much anything negative. *If it's negative, then it's their vibe.* You must not allow yourself to be this type of person. Instead, you should be the *solution generator*. Be the person who's there to give out suggestions. Be the person who analyzes the problem and then gives out well thought-out solutions to the problem.

Action Guide:

1 - Catch yourself spreading negative thoughts with other people. There's nothing wrong with sharing how bad your day is, but if you do it constantly, then people will get tired of you.

2 - Focus on giving out possible solutions.

3 - Practice generating solutions by making a list of 10 solutions to X.

Here's are some examples that you can do:

"Top 10 Solutions for being shy"
"10 things to do after a rejection"
"10 things to do before you sleep"

The point of this exercise is to test your idea muscle. The more you use it, the easier generating solutions become.

75 - Seek Assistance

It doesn't matter how good you are. It doesn't matter how if you're the best in the business. You are always going to need some assistance from other people.

The problem is too many people are full of pride. They live the motto of "If you want it done, then do it yourself," But you can only do so much. We all have the same 24 hours and ⅓ of that is even used for sleep.

So you cannot expect yourself to do everything.

Lower your pride and ask for help.

There's no shame in saying that you can't do it alone.

We need other people. The good news is they need us too!

"No man is an island, each connection is important."

Action Guide:

1 - Ask for someone's assistance. Evaluate all the repetitive things that you do every day and find a task that you can let others do.

2 - Outsource what you can outsource. Stop being a control freak and let other people do some of the work for you.

76 - Introduce People to Each Other (Be the Connector)

This is one of the most closely guarded secrets of the best connectors in different types of industries. The connectors are not selfish. In fact, the more people he introduces to each other, the better his life becomes.

Connecting people means introducing someone to another so they can make some kind of deal or connection. By being the connector, you're being the glue that sticks them together.

Doing this opens up lots of opportunities in different aspects of your life. By being the connector and introducing people to each other, you get to build a web of connection who value what each other brings to the table.

Action Guide:

Introduce a friend/business partner/colleague to someone whom you think they can help. Ask yourself, what does this person have to offer that can help the other party?

E.g.

Introduce a doctor to a friend who suffers from depression

Introduce a stock market investor to someone who wants to learn more about the business.

Introduce an investor to someone who needs capital for his start-up.

77 - Manage Your Emotions Well

Most of the tactics in this book are about managing yourself. If you look back at most of the chapters, they are mostly about you. It's not about controlling the other person. It's about presenting yourself in the best way possible.

Managing your emotions is the overarching concept that binds all of these together.

When you know how to manage your emotions - you get to build more self-confidence. Talking to other people gets easier, you get to have empathy for other people, you get to say the right things at the right time, and you get to have a relationship based on mutual respect.

Action Guide:

The best advice I can give you is to practice all the tactics in this book. They will give you a good foundation in making your "emotional management" skills - thus, helping you become a better version of yourself.

Conclusion

Improving and mastering your social skills is not easy. It requires tons and tons of effort, especially in the beginning.

Your commitment to getting better every day is something that you need to hold onto.

You cannot improve your social skills just by thinking about stuff. You need to apply what you learned in this book and test them in the real world. The action guide after each chapter can help you get started, so make sure that you implement them without judging the idea.

I cannot promise you that everything will go according to your way. The truth is, it probably won't. Mastering your social skills takes time and lots and lots of practice.

The good news is you can start small. You can start with a small action that will serve as the seed for improvement.

I wish you all the best in everything that you do.

Talk soon,

A.V. Mendez

OTHER BOOKS

The 45-Day Self Improvement Handbook: 45 Daily Ideas, Habits and Action-Plan for Becoming More Productive, Persuasive, Influential, Sociable and Self- Confident

Build Confidence & Self-Esteem: 90 Awesome Techniques to Become Confident, Overcome Self-Doubt, Shyness and Improve Your Self-Esteem

How to Focus: 54 Habits, Tools and Ideas to Create Superhuman Focus, Eliminate Distractions, Stop Procrastination and Achieve More With Less Work

Stop Procrastination & Increase Productivity: 60 Tricks on How to Improve Your Focus, Time Management, Habits, Productivity and Overall Ability to Get Things Done

I Need Your Help

Hey, did you like this book? Did you found it valuable and actionable? If so, kindly write a short review on Amazon. It would mean a lot to me. Reviews are the lifeblood of every author and the more reviews we get, the more people are likely to discover our work.

Thanks again and God bless you.

Printed in Great Britain
by Amazon

45786790R00078